DRAW, MODEL, & PAINT

PAINTING and COLORING DINOSAURS

by Isidro Sánchez
Illustrations by Vicenç Ballestar
Photographs by Juan Carlos Martínez

Gareth Stevens Publishing
MILWAUKEE

For a free color catalog describing Gareth Stevens' list of high-quality books,
call 1-800-542-2595 (USA) or 1-800-461-9120 (Canada).
Gareth Stevens' Fax: 414-225-0377.

Library of Congress Cataloging-in-Publication Data

Sánchez, Isidro.
   [Pinta dinosaurios. English]
   Painting and coloring dinosaurs / text by Isidro Sánchez ; paintings by Vicenç Ballestar ;
photography by Juan Carlos Martínez.
      p. cm. — (Draw, model, and paint)
   Includes index.
   Summary: Provides information about various kinds of dinosaurs and shows how to
use felt-tip pens, tempera paints, and crayons to make them.
   ISBN 0-8368-1517-3 (lib. bdg.)
   1. Tempera painting—Technique—Juvenile literature. 2. Drawing—Technique—
Juvenile literature. 3. Dinosaurs in art—Juvenile literature. 4. Dinosaurs— Juvenile
literature. [1. Tempera painting. 2. Drawing—Technique. 3. Dinosaurs in art.
4. Dinosaurs.] I. Ballestar, Vincenç, ill. II. Martínez, Juan Carlos, 1944- ill.
III. Title. IV. Series.
ND2440.S2513   1996
743'.6—dc20   95-45072

This North American edition first published in 1996 by
Gareth Stevens Publishing
1555 North RiverCenter Drive, Suite 201
Milwaukee, Wisconsin 53212, USA

Original edition © 1994 Ediciones Este, S.A., Barcelona, Spain, under the title
Pinta Dinosaurios. Text by Isidro Sánchez. Paintings by Vicenç Ballestar.
Photography by Juan Carlos Martínez. All additional material supplied for
this edition © 1996 by Gareth Stevens, Inc.

Series editor: Barbara J. Behm
Editorial assistants: Jamie Daniel, Diane Laska, Rita Reitci

Printed in the United States of America

1 2 3 4 5 6 7 8 9 99 98 97 96

CONTENTS

Media for painting and coloring

A medium is the material and style an artist uses. In this book, you will paint and color dinosaurs in three different media – felt-tip pens, tempera paints, and crayons. You will also discover fascinating details about the dinosaurs you create, such as when and where they lived, how big they were, what they ate, and how they defended themselves from enemies.

Felt-tip pens

Felt-tip pens hold colorful inks, and the tips come in various shapes. They have round tips or slanted tips.

Felt-tip pens also come in various thicknesses. Choose the thickness that best suits a project's needs.

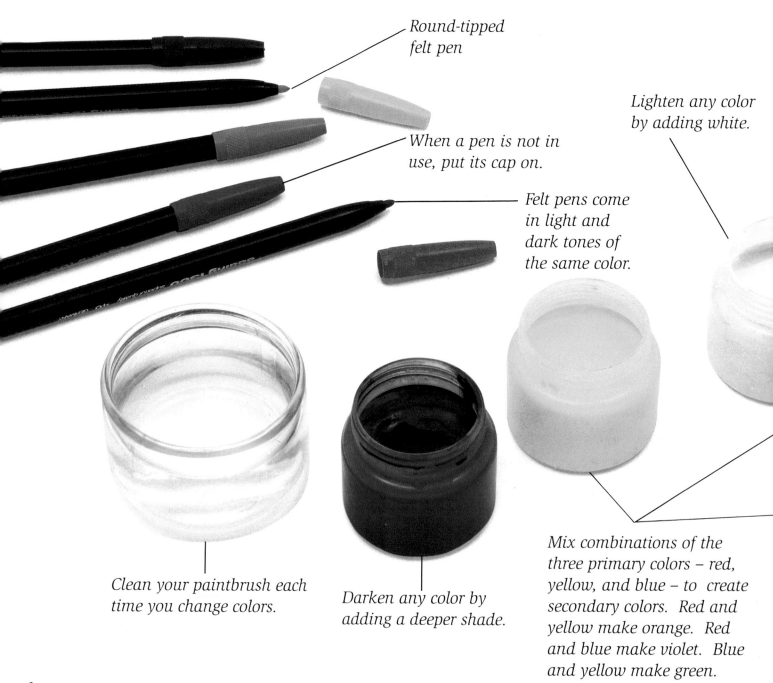

Round-tipped felt pen

Lighten any color by adding white.

When a pen is not in use, put its cap on.

Felt pens come in light and dark tones of the same color.

Clean your paintbrush each time you change colors.

Darken any color by adding a deeper shade.

Mix combinations of the three primary colors – red, yellow, and blue – to create secondary colors. Red and yellow make orange. Red and blue make violet. Blue and yellow make green.

4

Tempera paints

Tempera paints come in cakes, tubes, or jars in various vivid colors.

Painting with tempera is the oldest method of painting known to humans. Ancient peoples of Egypt, Babylonia, and Greece used hand-made tempera to make their wall paintings.

Crayons

Crayons are made of color pigment mixed with wax. Most sets of crayons contain the primary and secondary colors as well as lighter and darker tones of certain other colors. Choose your colors carefully because crayon cannot be erased!

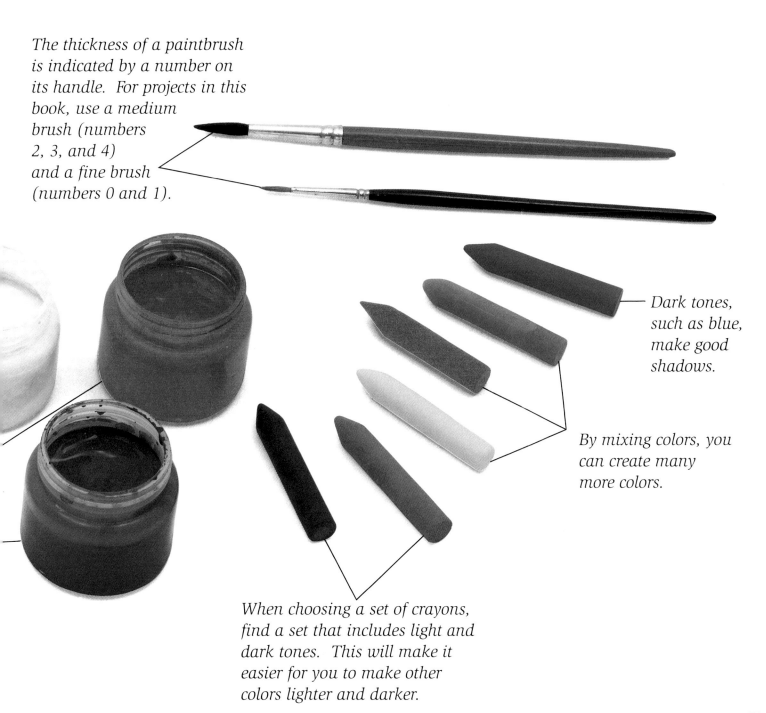

The thickness of a paintbrush is indicated by a number on its handle. For projects in this book, use a medium brush (numbers 2, 3, and 4) and a fine brush (numbers 0 and 1).

Dark tones, such as blue, make good shadows.

By mixing colors, you can create many more colors.

When choosing a set of crayons, find a set that includes light and dark tones. This will make it easier for you to make other colors lighter and darker.

Painting and coloring

Coloring with felt-tip pens

You can look right through the colors of felt-tip pens because their colors are transparent. See for yourself by making several lines with a dark-color pen, and then color over these lines with a light-color pen. You can still see the first lines through the new color.

If you color with the pointed tip of a pen, you will get a line as thin as the tip itself. If you color with the pen at an angle, you will get thicker strokes.

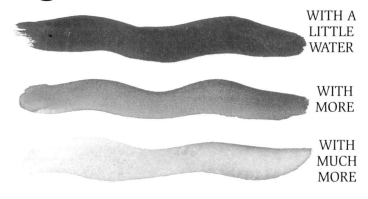

WITH A LITTLE WATER

WITH MORE

WITH MUCH MORE

Painting with tempera paints

Tempera is a water-based paint. Although one color can cover another, the paint can also be made transparent by adding water. Add the water, little by little, until you get the paint as thin as you want.

To mix two paints together, put them in a dish with some water and stir well.

To lighten a color, add white to it a little at a time until you get just the right shade.

To darken a color, add a darker color to it a little at a time until you get just the right shade.

Always wash your paintbrush in water before switching colors and upon completion of a project. Dry your brush with a cloth.

Let each color of your painting dry before applying the next.

Create a new color by combining two colors. If you color blue over yellow, you will get green.

1) COLOR YELLOW FIRST

2) COLOR BLUE OVER IT

3) THE RESULT IS GREEN

Coloring with crayons

It is easy to color with crayons. You don't need brushes or water. The colors mix easily, and you can blend or change colors you have already colored. Like tempera paints, crayons cover easily.

To get evenly colored areas, color lines closely together. Or you can draw them a little farther apart and then blend them by rubbing on them with your fingers. To make fine, or thin, lines, it is best to sharpen the tip of the crayon.

Tempera paints can be painted over one another. White can be painted over any dry color, even a dark one.

THE SHINY PART OF THIS APPLE WAS MADE BY PAINTING WHITE OVER A DARKER COLOR.

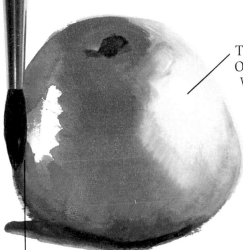

BY ADDING WATER, TONES CAN CHANGE.

LIGHTEN AN ALREADY-PAINTED COLOR WITH A DAMP BRUSH.

When mixing colors in a dish, blend them thoroughly with water until you get just the right color.

1   2

(1) Shade a color by gradually putting less pressure on the crayon. Then blend the color with your finger. (2) To mix two colors together, color one over the other, pressing down hard.

You can also color "in negative." Color a dark color over a light one, and then scrape the top color off in certain places with a toothpick.

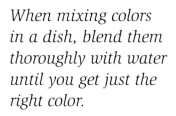

BEAUTIFUL PATTERNS CAN BE MADE BY SCRAPING CRAYON WAX AWAY.

A Torosaurus with felt-tips

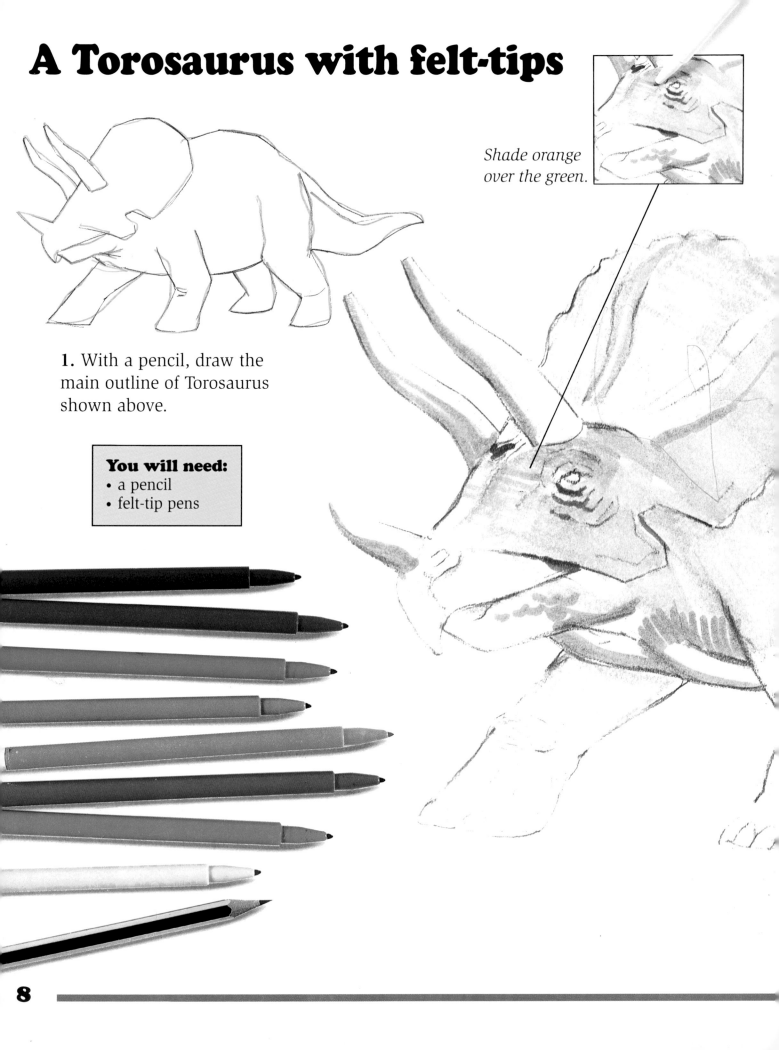

1. With a pencil, draw the main outline of Torosaurus shown above.

You will need:
- a pencil
- felt-tip pens

Shade orange over the green.

2. Draw in the details, such as the eyes and the folds of the skin.

3. Color areas as shown with an orange felt-tip pen. Slant the pen while coloring, and do not press too hard.

Your pencil lines indicate when to change colors.

4. Add light green and brown next to the orange base.

6. Shade the green part of the back by adding some pink lines. Darken the pink lines with brown.

5. Color the feet gray. Then add brown over the gray. Color some of the skin folds with the tip of your brown pen.

Hold your pen like this when darkening the outline.

7. Continue to darken the shadows and folds with brown. Draw in the lines running down the ridge on the dinosaur's back.

Name:
Torosaurus

When it lived:
70 million years ago

Size: 25 feet (7.6 meters) long

Where it lived: western areas of North America

Characteristics: This huge relative of Triceratops had an armored head and an enormous body. A large crest ran down its back. Big horns more than 3 feet (1 m) long grew from its eyebrows. It also had a big horn on its nose.

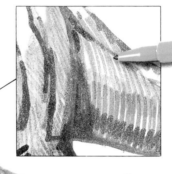

If you do the shading by drawing in lines, the ink can be controlled better.

8. Darken the outline of the entire dinosaur with brown. Add the final touches to the eye and the horns.

A Stegoceras with felt-tips

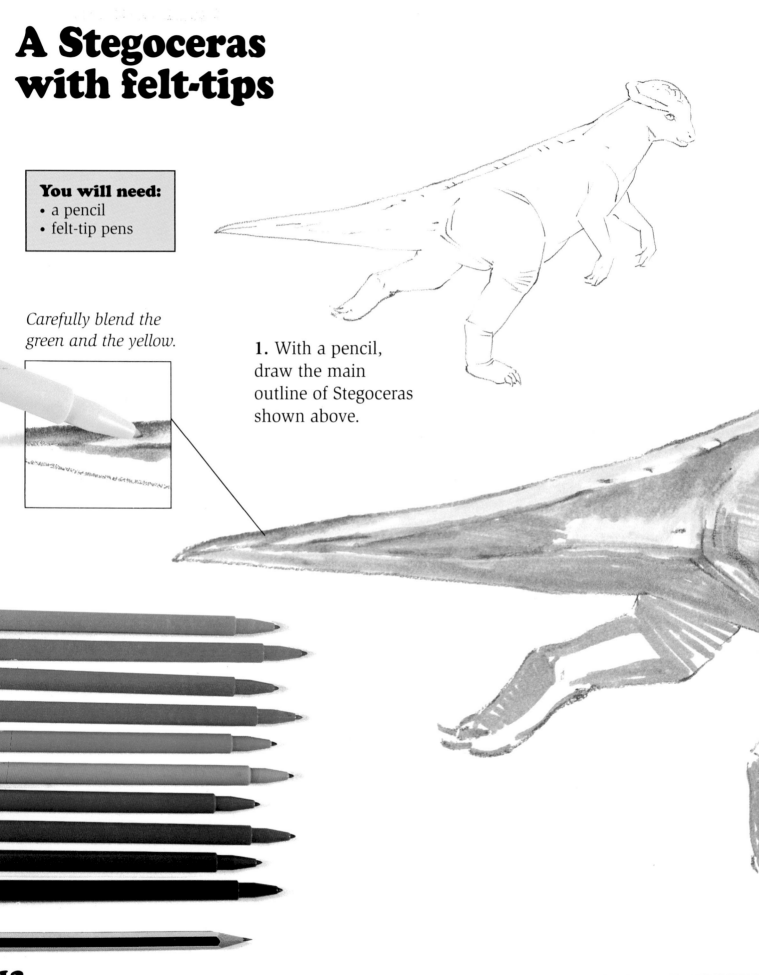

You will need:
- a pencil
- felt-tip pens

Carefully blend the green and the yellow.

1. With a pencil, draw the main outline of Stegoceras shown above.

2. Begin coloring with a light color, such as yellow.

3. Add light green to the dinosaur, as shown. Shade the feet by coloring in lines.

4. With an orange pen, color the stomach, under the tail, and areas of the legs and head.

Shade the stomach using individual lines.

13

6. Blend some red into the orange on the stomach and the underside of the tail. Go over the lines of the skin with dark green.

5. Add light green to the shaded lines on the legs.

With the yellow pen, carefully blend the edges of the two green areas together.

7. Use dark green to darken in shadows, especially on the neck, back, and feet. Add some quick "dabs" of dark green to make the markings on the skin.

8. Add light and dark brown to the shadows on the stomach and the underside of the tail. Use black to outline the folds of the skin and the crest on the head. Then outline the entire dinosaur with black.

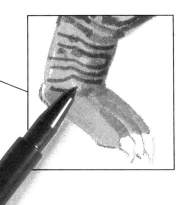

When outlining the folds in the skin, be sure your pen strokes are separated enough so it doesn't look like shading.

Name: Stegoceras

When it lived: About 75 million years ago

Size: 6-7 feet (1.9-2.2 m) long

Where it lived: North America

Characteristics: Stegoceras was very strong. It was a herbivore, or plant-eater. Stegoceras had a thick skull that looked like a helmet. Scientists think the males used these "hard hats" to butt heads with other males when they were competing for females. A male's skull was about 2.5 inches (6 centimeters) thick!

A Carnotaurus with crayons

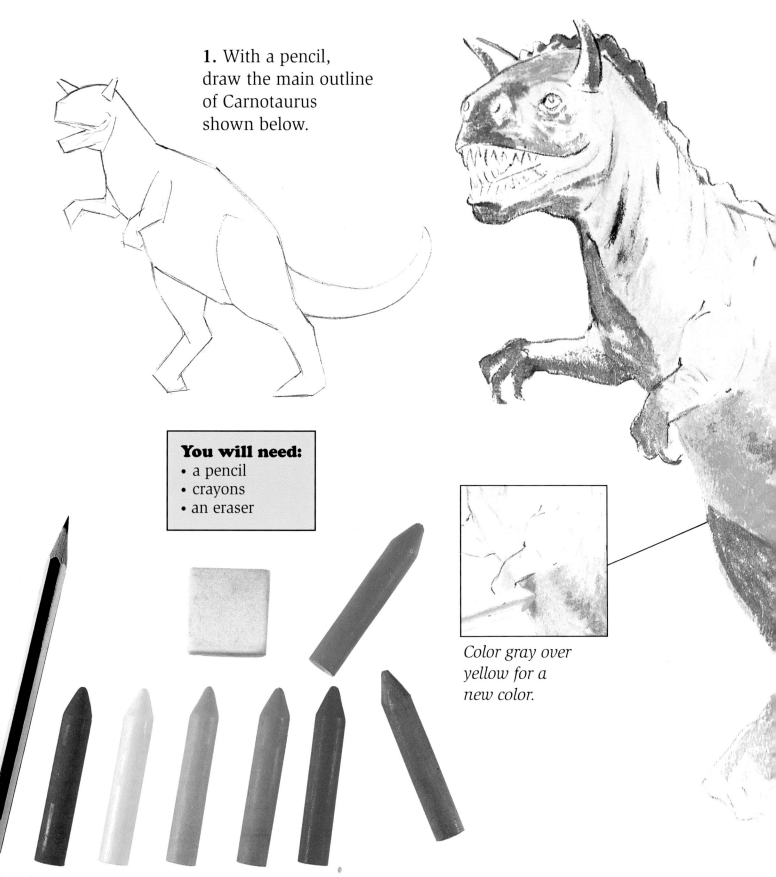

1. With a pencil, draw the main outline of Carnotaurus shown below.

You will need:
- a pencil
- crayons
- an eraser

Color gray over yellow for a new color.

2. Draw the eyes, teeth, horns, and claws. Add the other details shown, such as markings on the back and tail.

3. Begin to color with the yellow crayon.

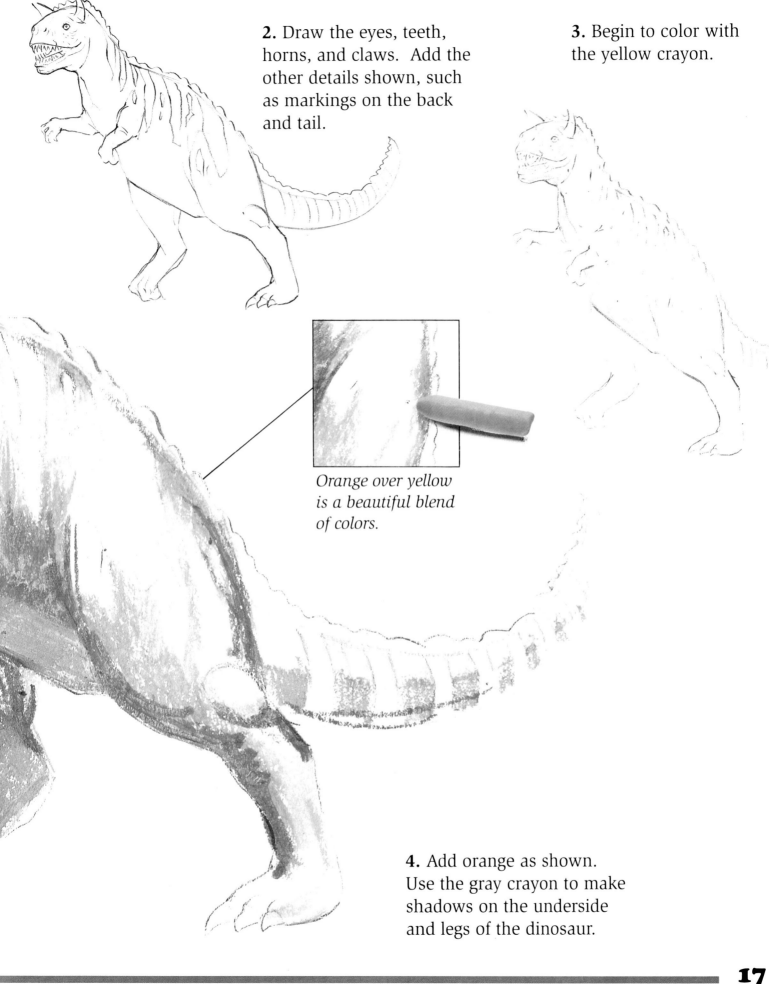

Orange over yellow is a beautiful blend of colors.

4. Add orange as shown. Use the gray crayon to make shadows on the underside and legs of the dinosaur.

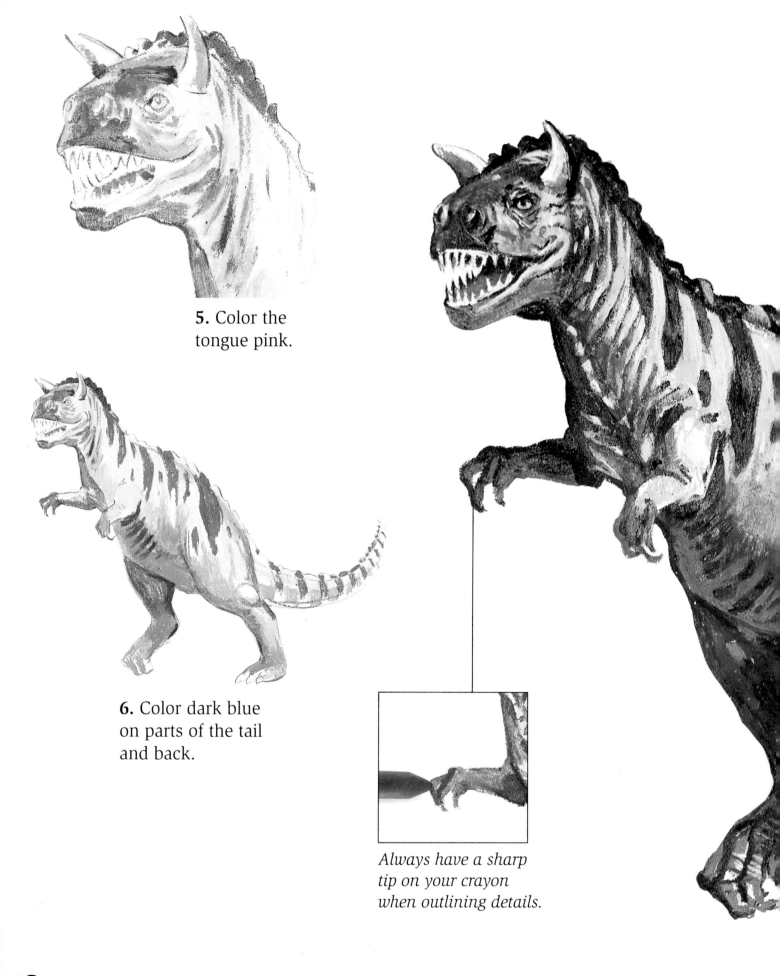

5. Color the tongue pink.

6. Color dark blue on parts of the tail and back.

Always have a sharp tip on your crayon when outlining details.

7. Add brown to the stomach and underside of the tail.

Add red over the blue on the back. Then go over it with blue to blend the colors.

8. Add red over the blue markings. Then color in the scales on the back, as shown, using a very sharp dark blue crayon.

9. Outline the back in dark blue. For the finishing touch, add some light blue to the back.

A Tyrannosaurus rex with crayons

1. With a pencil, draw the main outline of Tyrannosaurus rex shown at right. Add details to the head, claws, and legs.

Sharpen the tips of your crayons when you need to draw detailed lines.

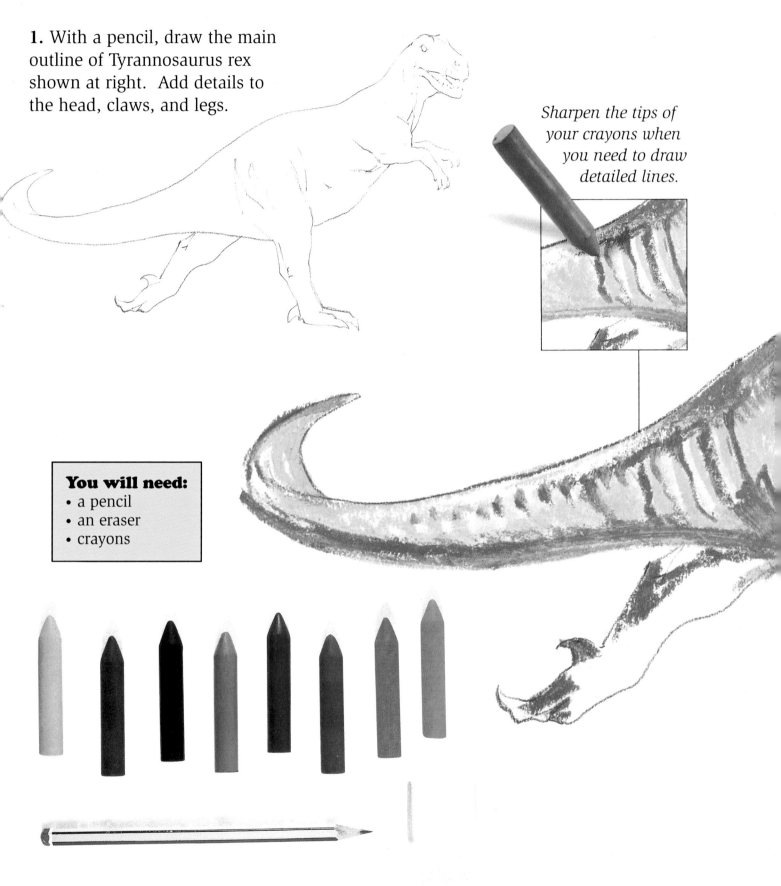

You will need:
- a pencil
- an eraser
- crayons

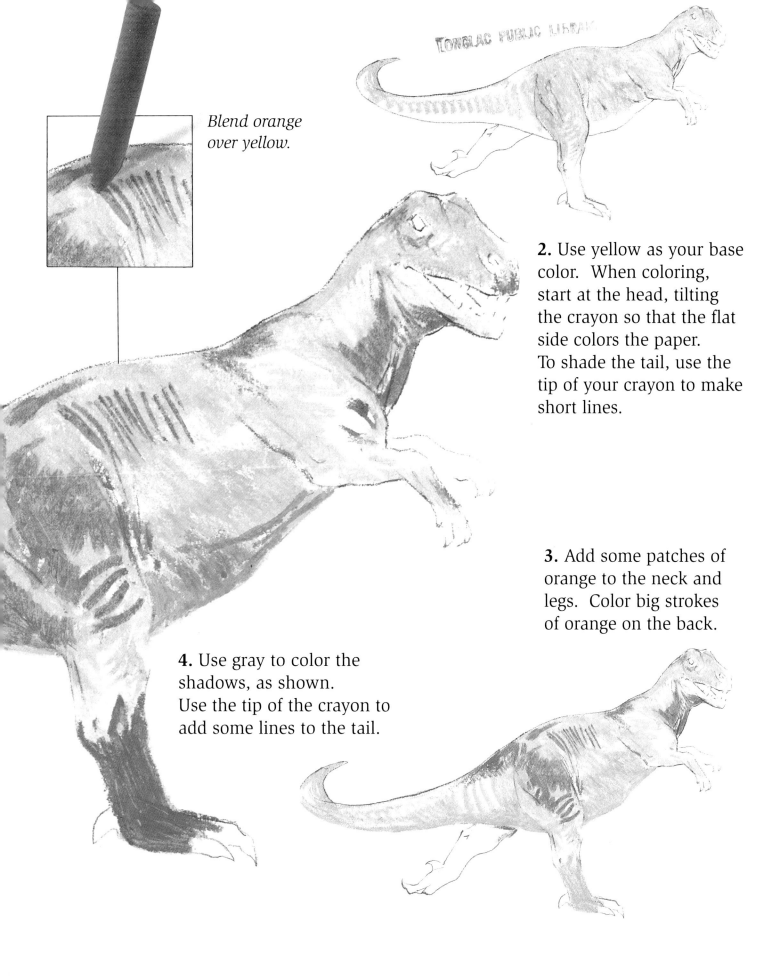

Blend orange over yellow.

2. Use yellow as your base color. When coloring, start at the head, tilting the crayon so that the flat side colors the paper. To shade the tail, use the tip of your crayon to make short lines.

3. Add some patches of orange to the neck and legs. Color big strokes of orange on the back.

4. Use gray to color the shadows, as shown. Use the tip of the crayon to add some lines to the tail.

7. Color in different directions with your crayons. It is a good way to fill in spaces.

6. Color the back legs dark red. Add dark brown to the tail.

5. Sharpen a bright red crayon. Use it to add highlights to the head, neck, back, tail, legs, and part of the stomach.

Name:
Tyrannosaurus rex

When it lived:
67 million years ago

Size: 46 feet (14 m)
long; 18 feet (5.5 m) tall

Where it lived: North America and Asia

Characteristics: This was one of the most ferocious carnivores that ever lived on Earth. When it found another dinosaur to prey upon, the prey rarely escaped. Each tooth of Tyrannosaurus rex was almost as big as a human hand. The teeth curved toward the inside of the mouth, so a victim was gripped with little chance of getting away.

9. Soften the black you have just added to the legs with red. Then go over the lines with gray, especially on the underside of the tail.

*Use strokes like
this to shade.*

*Add red over black
on the legs to soften
the black.*

8. Use black to color the shadows of the stomach and legs. Add a few strokes of dark green to the dinosaur's back.

A Gallimimus with tempera paints

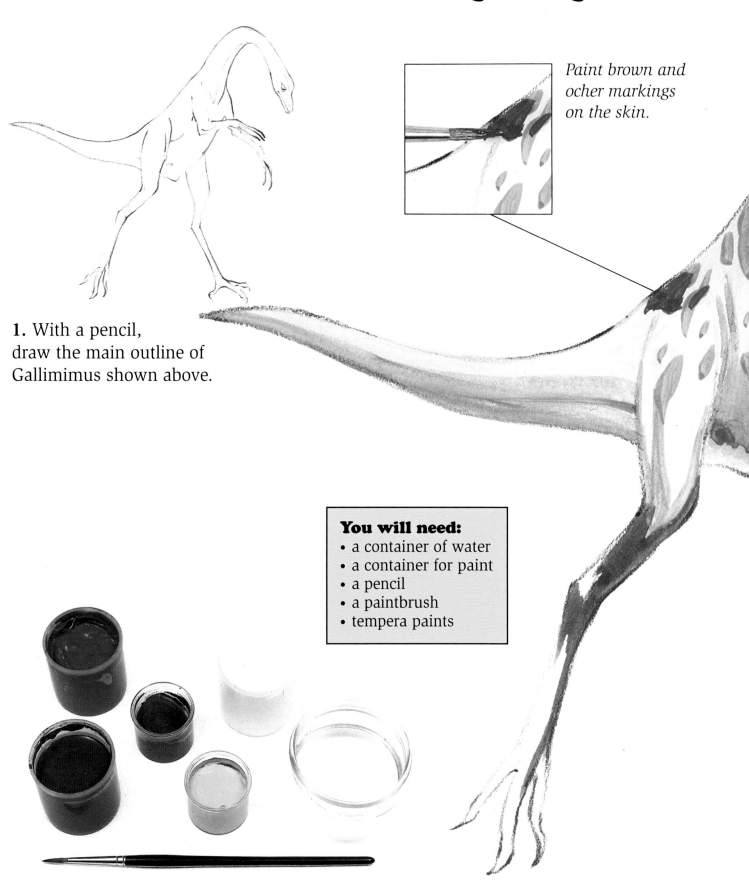

Paint brown and ocher markings on the skin.

1. With a pencil, draw the main outline of Gallimimus shown above.

You will need:
- a container of water
- a container for paint
- a pencil
- a paintbrush
- tempera paints

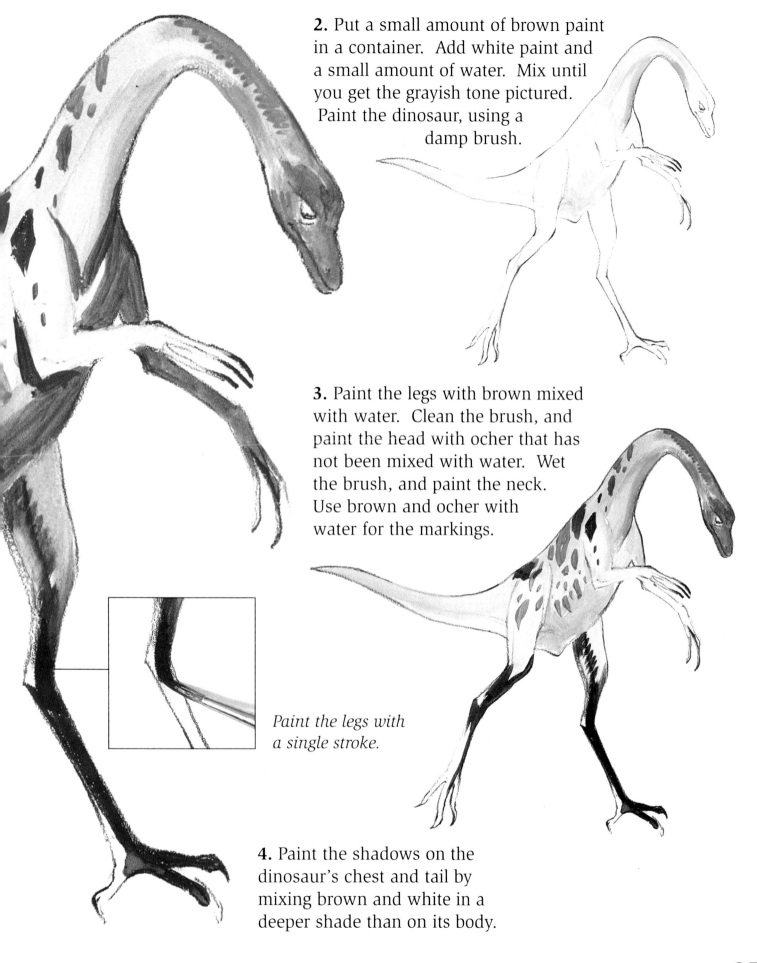

2. Put a small amount of brown paint in a container. Add white paint and a small amount of water. Mix until you get the grayish tone pictured. Paint the dinosaur, using a damp brush.

3. Paint the legs with brown mixed with water. Clean the brush, and paint the head with ocher that has not been mixed with water. Wet the brush, and paint the neck. Use brown and ocher with water for the markings.

Paint the legs with a single stroke.

4. Paint the shadows on the dinosaur's chest and tail by mixing brown and white in a deeper shade than on its body.

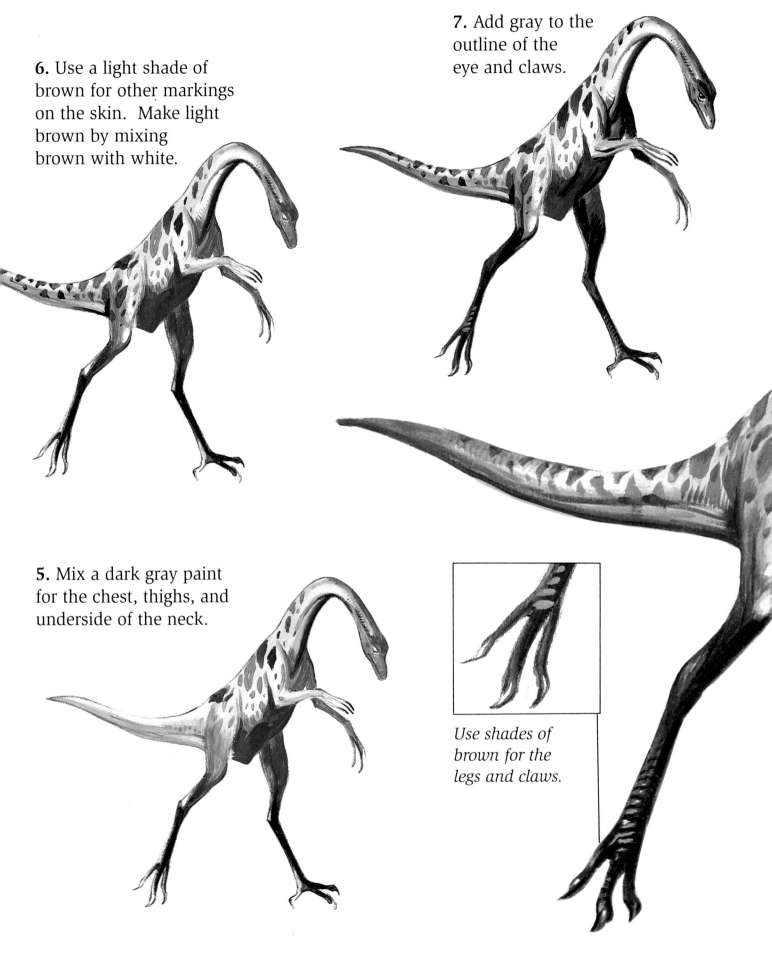

6. Use a light shade of brown for other markings on the skin. Make light brown by mixing brown with white.

7. Add gray to the outline of the eye and claws.

5. Mix a dark gray paint for the chest, thighs, and underside of the neck.

Use shades of brown for the legs and claws.

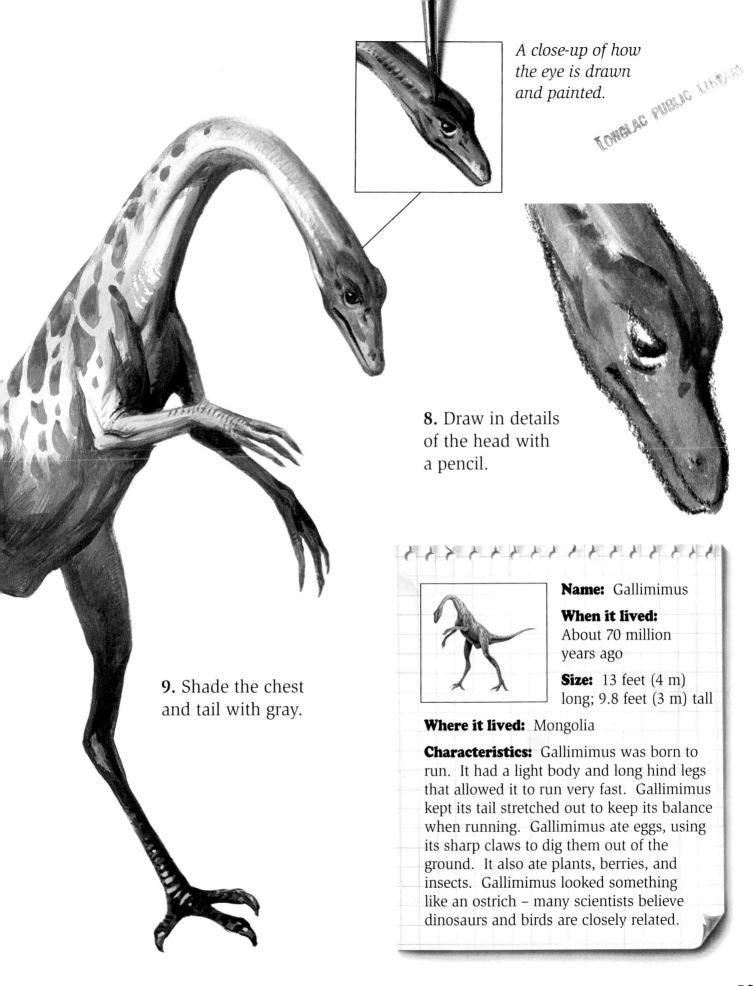

A close-up of how the eye is drawn and painted.

8. Draw in details of the head with a pencil.

9. Shade the chest and tail with gray.

Name: Gallimimus

When it lived: About 70 million years ago

Size: 13 feet (4 m) long; 9.8 feet (3 m) tall

Where it lived: Mongolia

Characteristics: Gallimimus was born to run. It had a light body and long hind legs that allowed it to run very fast. Gallimimus kept its tail stretched out to keep its balance when running. Gallimimus ate eggs, using its sharp claws to dig them out of the ground. It also ate plants, berries, and insects. Gallimimus looked something like an ostrich – many scientists believe dinosaurs and birds are closely related.

27

Diplodocus with tempera paints

Paint the inner neck areas blue.

1. With a pencil, draw the main outlines of the dinosaurs shown above.

You will need:
- a container of water
- a pencil
- a paintbrush
- tempera paints

You can paint a light color over a dark one with tempera paint.

2. Mix brown paint with white to get a grayish tone. Paint this color onto the outlines you have drawn, using a wet brush.

3. Paint a little ocher on the stomach. Add brown to the legs.

4. Make the two dinosaurs seem separate by painting watered-down blue onto the legs of the one in front, and onto the lower back of the one behind.

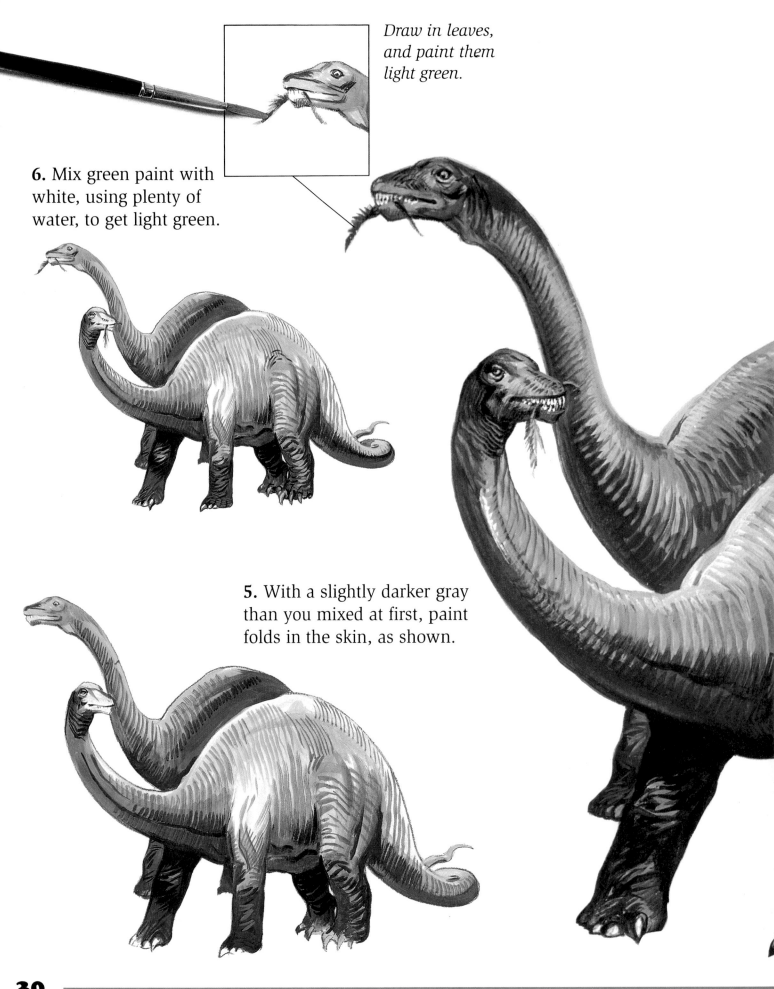

Draw in leaves, and paint them light green.

6. Mix green paint with white, using plenty of water, to get light green.

5. With a slightly darker gray than you mixed at first, paint folds in the skin, as shown.

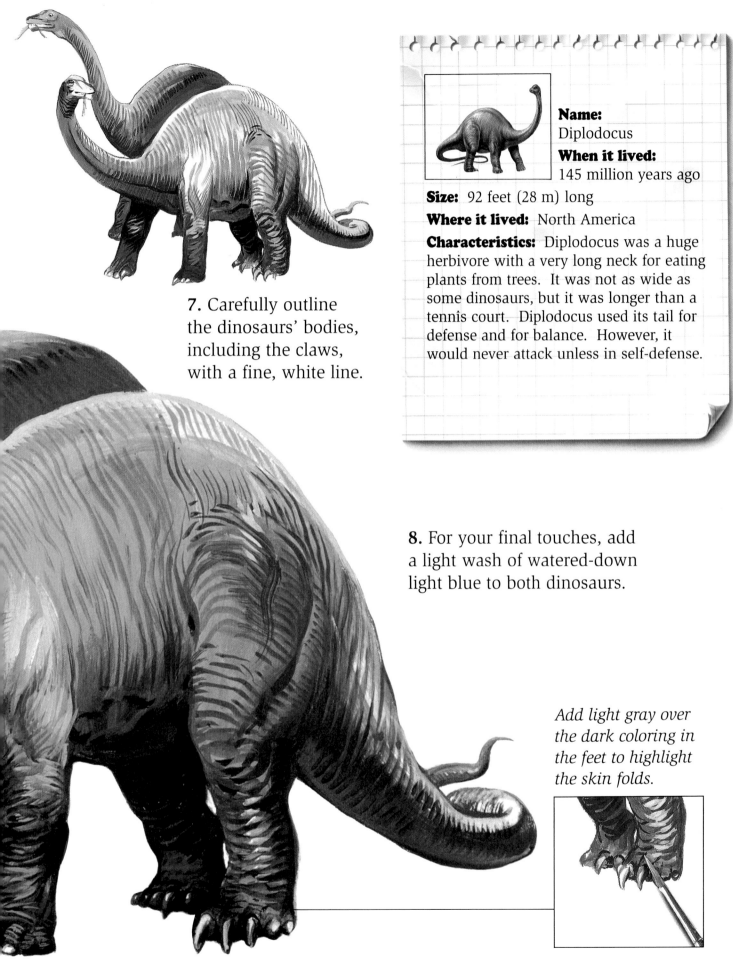

7. Carefully outline the dinosaurs' bodies, including the claws, with a fine, white line.

Name:
Diplodocus
When it lived:
145 million years ago

Size: 92 feet (28 m) long

Where it lived: North America

Characteristics: Diplodocus was a huge herbivore with a very long neck for eating plants from trees. It was not as wide as some dinosaurs, but it was longer than a tennis court. Diplodocus used its tail for defense and for balance. However, it would never attack unless in self-defense.

8. For your final touches, add a light wash of watered-down light blue to both dinosaurs.

Add light gray over the dark coloring in the feet to highlight the skin folds.

Glossary

blend: to mix substances so they cannot be separated again.

carnivore: an animal that eats meat as its primary source of food.

dinosaur: one of many varieties of huge land reptiles that once populated Earth but are now extinct.

herbivore: an animal that eats plant matter as its primary source of food.

media: a combination of styles, methods, and materials used by artists. Paint, crayons, chalk, and clay are media.

predator: an animal that hunts and eats other animals.

prey: an animal that is hunted and eaten by other animals.

primary colors: the basic colors that cannot be made from any other colors.

secondary colors: the colors made when two primary colors are mixed together.

tempera paints: paints that are mixed with water.

transparent: an object that is fine or sheer enough to see through.

Books and Videos For Further Study

Animals At A Glance: Dinosaurs & Other Prehistoric Animals. Flügel (Gareth Stevens)

The New Dinosaur Collection (series). (Gareth Stevens)

The New Dinosaur Library. Dixon (Gareth Stevens)

Worldwide Crafts (series). Deshpande and MacLeod-Brudenell (Gareth Stevens)

Dinosaur! Birth of a Legend: Tale of an Egg. (A&E Home Video)

The Infinite Voyage: The Great Dinosaur Hunt. (Vestron Video)

Index